Read
Critically

SUPER
QUICK
SKILLS

Read
Critically

Alex
Baratta

Los Angeles | London | New Delhi
Singapore | Washington DC | Melbourne

Los Angeles | London | New Delhi
Singapore | Washington DC | Melbourne

SAGE Publications Ltd
1 Oliver's Yard
55 City Road
London EC1Y 1SP

SAGE Publications Inc.
2455 Teller Road
Thousand Oaks, California 91320

SAGE Publications India Pvt Ltd
B 1/I 1 Mohan Cooperative Industrial Area
Mathura Road
New Delhi 110 044

SAGE Publications Asia-Pacific Pte Ltd
3 Church Street
#10-04 Samsung Hub
Singapore 049483

Editor: Jai Seaman
Assistant editor: Lauren Jacobs
Production editor: Tanya Szwarnowska
Marketing manager: Catherine Slinn
Cover design: Shaun Mercier
Typeset by: C&M Digitals (P) Ltd, Chennai, India
Printed in the UK

Library of Congress Control Number: 2019951130

British Library Cataloguing in Publication data

A catalogue record for this book is available
from the British Library

ISBN 978-1-5297-1335-0

At SAGE we take sustainability seriously. Most of our products are printed in the UK using responsibly
sourced papers and boards. When we print overseas we ensure sustainable papers are used as measured
by the PREPS grading system. We undertake an annual audit to monitor our sustainability.

Contents

Everything in this book!

Section 1   What is critical reading?

Your thoughts are yours only, until you go public with them as part of assessments. It's important to reveal how you interpret the subject based on having first done some careful reading of it.

Section 2   What does it mean to be critical?

We use our critical thinking skills in the real world without much effort. While this is easy to do with subjects we enjoy or are familiar with, it's exactly the same approach in university.

Section 3   How can I understand the assignment question?

Reading the assignment brief is easy to do and won't take long. But this is merely the start – you need to read carefully, taking apart the key words and then deciding what it all really means.

Section 4   How do I get from critical reading to critical writing?

The evidence of critical thinking is critical writing, putting your thoughts down for your assessment. Here you will learn how to communicate your thoughts effectively.

Section 5   Are there different ways to understand interpretation?

Interpretation comes in many forms and is what criticality is all about. Agreeing, disagreeing, illustrating and explaining are four ways to interpret the source material and prove you know what you're talking about.

Section 6   What is critical language?

How can you make your writing sound critical? Beyond the interpretation of the source material, there is also the need for appropriate language.

Section 7   How do I know I'm ready for the next assignment?

A run-through, where you can take the skills gained and apply them to an exercise involving the three stages of criticality: reading – thinking – writing.

Section 8   Where do I go from here?

Here is a final reminder of what being critical is all about – something to take away for all your future assessments, consisting of several activities.

What is critical reading?

10 second summary

Critical reading is all about interpreting the source material, in turn coming up with your own original ideas.

60 second summary

The need to be critical

Before we get to critical reading, let's start with critical thinking. Why? Because this is the term that gets shoved in your face from the moment you arrive at university, as opposed to critical reading. There is no doubt that being critical overall is the most important skill to demonstrate in your academic assessments, whether your assessment is an essay, exam or group presentation. However, there is not always enough explanation of what being critical actually means. While this guide will therefore explain criticality on three levels – reading, thinking and writing – it is indeed critical reading that is often the starting point.

> 'Critical reading gives birth to critical thinking.'

Understanding universities' use of the term 'critical thinking'

Critical thinking is a bit problematic as a term for two reasons:

1   First, the term suggests that the focus is all about what goes on in your head, but your lecturers can't see your thoughts of course. Thus, in terms of recognising your ability to be critical, lecturers can't read your mind. The evidence of your ability to be critical is housed in what you write, as part of an exam or essay, or occasionally in terms of what you say, as part of a group, or individual, oral presentation.

2   Second, and most relevantly, the ability to be critical often begins with critical reading as mentioned – we need to read a text first in order to generate the critical thinking. And it is critical reading, which leads to critical thinking, which then leads to critical writing – as part of your assessment on which you will be marked. So you might want to start regarding critical thinking as the

Assessment The means by which your knowledge of a subject is tested at university, including essays, exams and oral presentations, for example.

Criticality This is largely the same as analysis above, involving the need for close reading, probing for meaning and leading to the presentation of your own insights and interpretation.

Critical reading The act of not just reading a text, but asking questions about it – the implications for the claims it makes, considering examples of such claims and overall, trying to come to a central point – an interpretation – of the content.

academic middle-man that rests in between critical reading and the finished product, when you display your criticality in terms of what you produce for your

assessment. By reading your academic textbooks and journals carefully, you can then start to ponder what you've read and dissect it – thus, thinking critically – and the insights gained from this second step clearly lead to critical writing – that which the lecturer will see in an essay or exam.

Points to remember about being critical

- The previous points are not meant to present a one size fits all approach, however, regarding the route to being critical. You can read a chapter in your textbook and come up with nothing particularly critical, even after an hour of much effort.

- On the other hand, you might be on your way out to meet friends for dinner and then suddenly, without warning (and when you least expect it), inspiration strikes and you come up with a brilliant insight that you know will work well for your upcoming assessment.

- Thus, while you can sometimes appear to bypass the critical reading stage and instead jump straight to critical thinking, I would still suggest that many times, inspiration that otherwise seems to come out of nowhere, probably came from *somewhere* – often a product of the reading you did at some point, or certainly based on the class discussion you were involved with. Again, we need a starting point for our critical thinking – and this is critical reading.

- Inspiration cannot be forced, but you can achieve it. Moreover, by approaching the subject step by step as this guide does, then you will have the skills you need to approach being critical in a systematic way.

Reading versus *critical* reading

Read – **just read** – the following sentence:

> A proposal was made in 2018 to tow an iceberg from Antarctica to Cape Town in order to combat the drought there, which had resulted in a lack of water.

OK, now **analyse** the same sentence – i.e. read it *critically*:

> A proposal was made in 2018 to tow an iceberg from Antarctica to Cape Town in order to combat the drought there, which had resulted in a lack of water.

Now consider the following prompts (however obvious some might be):

- How could an iceberg combat water scarcity?

- Do you agree or not with this suggested solution – either way, explain why.

- If you disagree, are there other solutions to consider?

- What about the potential costs involved with transporting an iceberg?

- Might we consider ways that this crisis could have been prevented, whether in Cape Town or elsewhere?

- Could Cape Town's relative proximity to Antarctica make this a potential solution for this city in particular, but not others?

Granted, these are my prompts and you need to consider your own as the means to then generate your own insights. Nonetheless, the prompts give you some idea as to what you need to do. Reading critically leads to you thinking critically and then finally, providing evidence of both in your assessment, whether written (essay/exam) or spoken (an oral presentation). I suggest taking my prompts and running with them, jotting down some notes perhaps, even bullet points, which take things to the next level in terms of how the prompts are interpreted.

A student told us

'If you can be critical about the ingredients in your food, then you can be critical about academic theory.'

What does it mean to be critical?

10 second summary

Being critical means bringing something new to the table of academic discussion, largely by having first truly analysed, understood and interpreted the source material.

60 second summary

Reading is only the start

Reading is easy, but so is critical reading. The difference is that critical reading takes more time because it involves extra work once the reading is otherwise over. Once the reading is over, you then have to interpret what you have just read. This is true for an individual sentence as much as an entire book chapter. Once you get into this habit, it will become second nature. So from now on, take the time needed to carefully consider what you read and use the following question to help jump-start the process of critical reading: 'What does this text mean to *me*?'

Being critical is not just tied to school – it's everywhere

The question posed as this section's title is often the question on students' lips and I can answer it very easily. Being critical is firmly based on two factors – **interpretation** and **thinking for yourself**. It really is that simple. Putting the two together, it means that you must:

Interpretation Coming up with your own opinions based on the content of the text you've read.

- interpret what you read;

- ensure that the interpretations you arrive at are indeed yours.

In other words, the easiest way to be very *un*critical within your university assessments is to ensure that your responses for the exam or essay question are a cut and paste of what your lecturer told you in class and/or class handouts. This means that an interpretation, as a means to being critical, is only valid if it is indeed yours and yours alone. I didn't say that you should never refer to lecture notes/class discussion/board diagrams/the lecturer's PowerPoint material in your assessments. Rather, refer to such merely as a springboard to then launching your own interpretation of the exam/essay/assessment question(s).

After all, how can you be critical when the only interpretations you use in an assessment belong to someone else?

'Being critical does not mean criticising – it means stopping to think about what you've just read or seen.'

Real-world critical reading

Let's start with a simple exercise, involving the analysis of the bolded sentence below which references *Star Wars*. Do not think that just because the sentence is reflective of pop culture, that it is not 'academic' enough. Critical thinking is not just needed for academia anyway. We use our analytical abilities on a daily basis, whether young or old, whether on campus or on holiday. The approach we take is exactly the same – whether analysing a textbook or a hotel's online amenities. And the approach is this: **read, ponder** and **interpret**.

Analysis The act of investigating key words (for texts) and the overall meaning derived, in order to find a deeper meaning and/or the implications of the text.

Critical thinking The act of pondering over the text as you read, or after reading, in order to reach an overall interpretation.

Interpreting Star Wars

Whether you like *Star Wars* or not, the content of the sentence below is simple enough. Reading the sentence below is equally simple. But reading is not enough if you want to be critical. You need to interpret the content, so have a think about it and jot down some interpretations, of any length, in terms of what the content of the sentence means to you.

In the current trilogy of *Star Wars* films produced by Disney, we now find a great deal more racial diversity than in the original trilogy from 1977–1983.

Interpretation 1: _____

Interpretation 2: _____

Interpretation 3: _____

Here are some I came up with:

Interpretation 1: Such racial diversity is reflected in the real world, so it makes sense that the film world might wish to reflect this also for the modern generation of cinema-goers.

Interpretation 2: Given Disney's desire to show more racial diversity (e.g. *The Princess and the Frog*), then perhaps it is unsurprising that this ethos is reflected in a major film franchise.

Interpretation 3: As there was some criticism of a largely white galaxy in the original *Star Wars* trilogy, perhaps Disney wishes to finally address this.

Regardless of which interpretation you like best, if any, all that matters is that you can agree that the three sentences directly above are logical extensions of the original sentence. Do not make the mistake of thinking that my interpretations are somehow 'better' than yours. This is not about right or wrong. Rather, it is simply about interpreting what you read and coming up with your own interpretation, and not passing someone else's interpretation off as yours. As you can see, being critical is not just reflected in your reading and subsequent processing of the reading (as part of critical thinking); it's also reflected in how you *communicate* criticality, here in writing.

Interpreting a scene from a film

'Academic reading' and 'reading a film' are not about reading per se and more accurate ways to conceive of reading here are 'academic (textbook) analysis' and 'analysing a film'. Analysis, then, is the key word and it can be extended to much more than the printed words on a page. But once again, the approach to analysis is the same regardless of the source – you need to interpret the source material, whatever that may be.

Let's have a look using a scene from the movie *American Beauty* (1999):

Description

In this early scene, the character of Carolyn Burnham (Annette Bening) is gardening and stops to admire a bright red rose, amidst a large well-kept garden surrounded by a white picket fence.

Analysis

In this early scene, the character of Carolyn Burnham (Annette Bening) is gardening and stops to admire a bright red rose, amidst a large well-kept garden surrounded by a white picket fence. The connotations of the white picket fence arguably reflect peace and tranquillity, having succeeded in achieving the American dream of owning her own home and having a comfortable middle-class lifestyle. Given that Bening is displaying a large smile as she admires her rose, we might believe that she is indeed happy and content. However, the overall effect of the bright white picket fence, a somewhat forced smile and a rose that is very red and bright indeed all create a sense of visual irony; her life is actually quite dark. The white picket fence alone connotes happiness, but director Sam Mendes goes on to show us that these suburban families are anything but happy, trapped in some sort of existential crisis.

You can clearly see the difference between the two examples. Don't get hung up on the difference in length, however. Indeed, uncritical writing can go on and on forever, and end up filling a page or more. It's about quality.

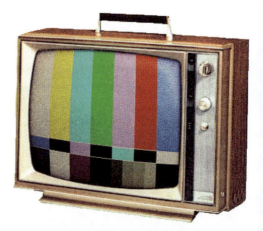

Tip!

- Whatever the source material is – a book, journal article, aroma, film, architectural style, item of clothing and so on and so on – stop to ponder it before you write a word.

- Ask yourself, 'what does this mean to me?'

- Provide your subsequent interpretation BUT:

  ○ make sure the interpretation is indeed yours;

  ○ use cautious language (e.g. perhaps, this suggests that...; the implications might be.....);

  ○ always ensure that you provide an illustration to follow an otherwise broad word or expression – don't leave it to the reader to do the illustrating for you as they read – and mark – your assessment.

A student told us

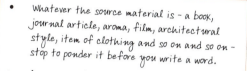

'Learn to analyse the obvious things around you – even the display of food in the school canteen – and you're on the right track to critical thinking in assessments.'

ACTIVITY How to critically read images

Consider a famous painting, such as the Mona Lisa, or simply a favourite photograph you have.

First, write down what you see in the painting/photograph.

....

....

From there, and taking the same visual, what do you *really* see? In other words, write a short paragraph interpreting the detail in the visual and what this connotes to you – the colours, the positioning of objects within the picture, the expressions and so on.

....

....

....

....

....

The purpose of this brief exercise is once again to mimic what we do on a daily basis when we're out and about in the real world, even without any educational context to be seen. Our mind is capable of processing information very quickly, to include making quick judgements of a picture, building, movie poster, menu design and so on. Once again, take that skill that you already have and transfer it to your academic texts.

CHECK POINT How do you feel about the concept of being critical?

Based on the question above, give yourself a score from 0 (very low) to 5 (very high) regarding the statements below:

Score

I understand the rationale for being critical in
my assessments. ☐

I can define 'criticality' (e.g. critical reading/thinking)
confidently in my own words. ☐

I could explain critical thinking to someone else so they
would understand. ☐

If my previous academic work was in any way *un*critical,
I now know where I went wrong. ☐

I feel more confident now to approach my next
assignment with regard to being critical. ☐

Congratulations

By now, you should have confidently acquired the crux of being critical, the ability to think for yourself based on:

- interpreting the source, whatever that might be;
- coming up with your own original ideas and not relying on someone else's;
- that's it!

How can I understand the assignment question?

10 second summary

An assignment question must be broken down word by word, unpacking each word in turn, to arrive at an overall understanding of the question, and not merely 'reading' it.

60 second summary

Never read an assignment question – analyse it!

Understanding the question set for your essay, exam or oral presentation (or any other kind of assessment), is vital. Simply reading the question won't be enough. You again need to analyse it, as the means to dig deeper, and having done so, arrive at a clear and deep understanding of what you need to do. Some lecturers will effectively do the work for you, presenting you with a question which is deconstructed for you, complete with a list of specific theories/authors/topics to focus on. You might prefer this approach, compared with an approach which is more minimal, providing you with little more than a few sentences consisting of the question that you must then deconstruct. Either way, be prepared to use some DIY for assessment questions.

Critically reading an assignment question

Reading critically begins with the assignment question. After all, this is the starting point for what will be an eventual essay, exam or presentation. Let's now practise with a sample question:

Discuss the implications of social media on students' relationships with their friends

You've already read the sentence above. Easy, wasn't it? It probably took less than five seconds. But critical reading takes more time than this. It requires you, once again, to take a step back and interpret the question. You probably already know that the first step in analysing an assessment question is to highlight the key words – this alone requires critical reading skills, so that you can discern which words are key and which are not. It is from analysis of this one sentence that the quality of your essay/exam will rest. Thus, an essay of 1,500 words, for example, can begin life as nothing more than just one sentence. Let's get started:

Discuss – This is a very common word used in academic circles, along with 'analyse' and 'critically discuss'; they all refer to the same thing. So what does 'discuss' mean in academia? On a simple level, it means ensuring that you spend the necessary time explaining the subject, but going deeper, it means that you have to show both sides of the coin – you need to explain the good and the bad with regard to the implications of social media on students' relationships with their friends. Moreover, it's important that you present equal coverage for both sides. So if writing a 1,500-word essay, for example, you would want to make sure that you spend a similar amount of discussion for both sides; this might mean having two paragraphs discussing the pros, and two paragraphs discussing the cons. If you instead devoted three paragraphs which focused on the benefits and only one paragraph focused on the negative side (or vice versa), then this might come across as biased.

Some potential pros and cons of social media on students' relationships are provided:

Pros

Easy to keep in touch

A good means to share ideas for homework

Cons

Can lead to bullying, even amongst friends

Children can become too obsessed about their phones, texting, likes, etc.

We can go even further, by critically reading the content of the above pros and cons:

Pros

Easy to keep in touch, **so this allows for many benefits. Students can be in close contact if they need to talk about personal issues with their friends.**

A good means to share ideas for homework, **which enables students to develop online study groups, for example, and learn from each other using a medium of communication they're comfortable with.**

Cons

It can lead to bullying, even amongst friends. *This can sometimes start with an innocent comment taken the wrong way and given the instant nature of texting, for example, soon many other friends join the conversation.*

Children can become too obsessed about their phones, texting, likes, etc. *This can take away from face-to-face communication, perhaps leading to a lack of social skills in the process.*

At this point, we're essentially throwing ideas on the canvas, and seeing where we can go from there. This may later involve a great deal of deleting, revising, tweaking, polishing and so on. But as you can see, a start has been made.

Implications – The very nature of this word means that nothing is definite. To imply something is not the same as saying it outright. It is less certain. Likewise, the fact that the essay/exam question has asked you to discuss 'implications' means that you need to tread carefully when discussing the various topics related to social media use by students. I've already mentioned the need to use cautious language within your writing, but here it is especially relevant given this one word alone.

Also, the 'implications' of anything do not inherently point toward positive or negative. Instead, implications can be both. Once again, this is telling you, albeit indirectly, that you need to focus on the pros and cons regarding social media usage.

You might wonder why the lecturer didn't simply spell all this out for you, and provide a full page of instructions for your assessment. Well, some lecturers will do this, of course, and some students prefer this approach, while others don't. After all, to have too much detail about an assignment can lead to some students not knowing where to start. More than this, however, if someone does it for you, in terms of breaking down the assignment question into all its inherent parts, then developing your own critical reading – and thinking – skills has been lost.

Social media – These two words lead to a very broad concept indeed. There are so many examples of social media out there, many of which you may be involved with yourself. However, did the essay specify that you need to focus on a particular kind of social media? It didn't. Does this mean, then, that you are free to choose any kind of social media to discuss? It depends. Look at the question carefully. It's asking you to focus on the kinds of social media that students are using. This will require a degree of speculation – itself tied to being critical – because you will need to choose those media that are perhaps most popular nowadays with students. Facebook and Twitter come to mind, but there could be others to focus on. Ultimately, the kinds of research that have already addressed this subject would be those to consider if you're stuck, as there must be academic papers/books out there which have discussed particular social media that are common with students nowadays.

Other things to consider:

- Media is plural of course (medium is the singular), though how many examples would you choose to focus on? The question doesn't specify so you have to be critical even here, by deciding on how many is just right for an exam question or for a 1,500 word essay. Clearly, one type of media would not be enough, based on the question alone.

- Would you define social media as part of your background information? Again, the question does not require you to, so you don't have to. But thinking critically, might a definition help to orient the reader to this subject that bit better, perhaps as part of background information in the introduction paragraph?

Students – This is another broad word, as 'students' could be realized on many levels, from primary (elementary) school all the way to postgraduate education. Once again, the question does not specify a particular educational level so this means it is indeed up to you to decide what level of education you wish to focus on. However, it would make sense to choose a level of education that you believe is particularly pertinent to this topic.

On the other hand, you could also focus on several levels of education within your assessment, in order to provide a broad overview of the situation. There are many, many potential ways this could unfold – and it's up to you – but below is an example:

- Messaging amongst primary (elementary) school students.

- Facebook use amongst high school students.

- Twitter use amongst university students.

Whether you focus on one education level throughout, or a combination, the most relevant factor is that there is, and has been, some clear impact on students' relationships with friends with regard to social media usage. You may of course even have your own ideas on this and some personal experience. Use those as a starting point, but of course make sure that you refer to the relevant literature on this, which may indeed illustrate some of the issues – good and bad – within the use of Facebook, Twitter and so on.

Going even deeper, did you consider why the focus is on students per se within the assessment brief (and not, for example, on 'individuals')? Why focus on students? To answer this question once again requires some analysis, but it's analysis that led to the question being posed in the first instance, in terms of the lecturer's decision to focus on students.

Consider the possibilities as to why students might make for a relevant focal group for an assignment focused on social media:

- Within the context of education – including the classroom level – perhaps effects on relationships with one's peers are more visible (e.g. in-groups, out-groups).

- A negative effect might be less engagement with one's school work, as social media is taking up more time.

- On the other hand, teachers' use of social media as a teaching tool can be a very accessible means for students to learn a variety of subjects (e.g. by using YouTube).

- Bullying is indeed something that schools take seriously and try to weed out; the use of social media to spread rumours about a student is one example of online bullying.

- The use of messaging can also be an effective means to send instant greetings, condolences, encouragement and so on to one's classroom friends – so a positive use.

These are just five potential examples, but see if you can construct more and in doing so, have a variety of potential topics to discuss which would combine to address the question.

Relationships (with their) friends – Clearly, the focus is on platonic, not romantic, relationships. If this distinction seems unnecessarily pedantic, it's not. Rather, it is based solely on what the question tells us, and it is the instructions for your assessments (whether in the form of a question or not) that must be adhered to. Don't forget that the score for your assessments rests entirely on how well you understand the question in the first place. And your understanding depends entirely on how well you analyse – and not just read – the question from the start.

'Be prepared to read your assignment question a dozen or more times to get it right.'

Summary

Make sure you pull apart, unpack and dissect each and every key word within the assignment brief, first determining what the key words are of course. This involves more than simply defining the words, as this is just the start. From here, make sure that you explore the *connotations* of the key words, as was discussed with the one word of 'implications' above. As mentioned, some lecturers might do much of this for you as part of a more detailed assignment brief, but you need to be prepared for instructions for assessments which otherwise require you to do the (critical) thinking.

CHECK POINT

How do you now approach assessment questions?

You've just gone through a sample assessment question, bit by bit. With this knowledge, answer 'true' or 'false' to the statements below – but feel free to state 'not applicable' if you think the statement is neither true nor false (this kind of answer would show that you're being critical!).

Circle your answer below:

Even prepositions (to, from), articles (a, the) and otherwise 'small' words within the assessment instructions could be key words.   *True / False*

Lecturers should provide all the details for me regarding assessment questions – it's not my job!   *True / False*

Some of the instructions might be stated indirectly, not directly, within the assessment brief.   *True / False*

ACTIVITY Create your own question

For this exercise, rather than analyse another question/assignment brief, create your own. Aim for one sentence, whether phrased as a question or as a statement. Consider each and every word you use, as if you were the lecturer setting this for an actual assessment.

Jot it down below:

....

....

....

....

....

....

....

....

....

A student told us →

'If you get the question wrong, then you've stumbled at the first hurdle.'

Congratulations

At this point, you should:

- understand the difference between reading and critical reading;

- understand how to actually do critical reading for an assignment brief;

- understand the two basic – yet crucial – elements of how to be critical: interpret the source material and ensure that your interpretation is indeed yours.

How do I get from critical reading to critical writing?

10 second
summary

Critical thinking is the middle man between reading and writing. Once you've collected your thoughts regarding the text, it's time to put these on the page.

60 second summary

Prove your critical thinking ability by putting it on the page

Lecturers can't read your thoughts, as I mentioned earlier, so make sure your critical thinking is realized as critical writing. You will indeed do a lot of reading once you get to university. Each course unit will have its own reading list, often divided into core reading, recommended reading and suggested reading. When you consider that a full-time load of course units might be about five course units a week, that equates to a great deal of reading. This involves academic textbooks in the main, but also academic journal articles and sometimes, websites on which you can find studies, statistics and links to government papers which are relevant to your subject of study.

Critically reading academic texts

Let's begin with an extract from an academic journal article. Granted, the subject represented in this chapter will not necessarily fit with your own. However, as I have stressed, being critical is the same no matter what you study, and practice in interpreting a subject which is not your own is good practice indeed. In other

Text The source material from which a critical reading – and understanding – derives, such as a book, journal article, painting, film, picture and so on.

words, if you can develop your interpretation skills for a subject that you don't study at university, then how much easier should this be for your own subject of study? The excerpt below is from the subject area of linguistics:

There is much literature on the study of teacher identity from a linguistic perspective, notably in the United States (Godley & Escher, 2012; Gutierrez & Orellana, 2006; Haddix, 2010, 2012; Reaser, 2016). A central issue concerns the dilemma sometimes faced by teachers who speak a variety of English deemed unsuitable for the teaching context. For example, Haddix (2012) references the 'mismatch' between African-American teachers' language and that expected within the classroom, based on language norms pertaining to White, middle-class women. Even for teachers who are otherwise perfectly qualified to teach, there can be a discrepancy between their home language and that expected within the classroom, as a result of dominant linguistic norms in education. This applies to native and non-native English speakers alike and within this paper, this phenomenon pertains solely to a teacher's accent, which, in some cases, can lead to prejudice.

Source: Baratta, 2017

The writing sample above is the first paragraph within a journal article. Conceivably, however, it could have come from any section of the article because the point is that critical reading of your academic texts can take place anywhere within the book, chapter, article, website and so on that you are reading.

> 'Critical thoughts lead to critical texts – prove your critical thinking ability by putting it on the page.'

Getting started with critical reading

Getting started, a good way to begin is to read the text and then ask, 'what does this mean to me?'. This does not mean that this question needs to be raised with each and every sentence you come across; to be honest, that would be both unnecessarily time-consuming and a bit artificial. Rather, I strongly suggest that you read the whole paragraph on the previous page and then ask the prompt regarding what it means to you. What it means to you of course may be very, or somewhat, different, from what it means to me. And while a single sentence in the paragraph may indeed shout out to you and that sentence alone might be the basis of your subsequent interpretation, for others the interpretation might instead be based on their overall impression, one that perhaps takes into account a bit of everything.

Now, have a look at some potential examples – here more than just a sentence – which derive from an understanding of the previous para-graph and then seek to interpret it. The question is not whether you agree or disagree with the interpretations; rather, do you agree with *the logic behind the interpretations?*

Interpretation One

Perhaps the United States, given a long history since its inception with a multitude of cultures – and subsequent languages – is more self-aware of the issues that can arise as a result. The dialect of Ebonics, spoken by some African-Americans, is a particular example of equating someone's language use with their intelligence, given the views toward Ebonics as being defective English or bringing 'the ghetto' into the classroom. Clearly, teachers need to use a variety of language that is considered appropriate for schooling, the variety often being Standard English. However, does this mean that teaching students about the use of non-standard forms is inherently wrong?

OK, if I were looking at the above paragraph, I would be satisfied that it is an example of critical writing – provided, as always, – that it's not merely quoting lecture notes or comments I made in class. If not, then this means it is reflective of the student's own interpretation, and while this may be inspired by what the student read in the first place perhaps, it is not a mere copy of what they read. This is because it brings something new to the table.

Interpretation Two

The teaching profession is one in which one's voice is of central importance. Students need to understand their teacher of course, and we would hope that teachers have an engaging tone, for example, one that suggests they enjoy their profession. However, there appear to be issues with certain uses of language by teachers within the classroom, which perhaps have little to do with being understood by students. Whether it is the use of certain dialects such as Ebonics, or various accents, such as broad regional accents in Britain, socio-cultural attitudes toward language varieties might be strongly felt, to the extent that they are, in effect, banned from the classroom. Our language use is a badge of identity and therefore, it is not necessarily the language per se that is the issue. Rather, it is what a given language variety connotes to those listening. As such, if a particular accent does not have positive connotations in society, then it perhaps won't enjoy such either within the classroom.

This is a different interpretation than the first one of course, but equally valid. Here, the writer is exploring the subject and in doing so, once again offering something new in the process. All good paraphrases should do this. Contrary to popular belief, a paraphrase is not just about saying the same thing as the original text, but with different words. The very fact that you are using different words in the first place means that you are saying something different from the original text anyway, no matter how slightly the words differ from the original. But a good paraphrase should bring out the 'hidden meaning' which the original author is communicating; this means reading between the lines which once again means analysing and not just merely reading.

In fact, if we go back to the original text, below are some bullet points which illustrate some additional ideas which derive from the text, though only gleaned with a close reading of it:

- Language prejudice can be a proxy for racial prejudice.

- Who decides what is or is not acceptable for the language a teacher uses, to include his/her accent?

- Teachers perhaps lack power to decide on their language use, but perhaps they should have more agency.

- We are all different and diversity is something that is celebrated, and protected, in modern society; why should this not be reflected in the classroom?

- If students hear teachers who have the same accent as them, this can help empower students, and even help them envisage a career in teaching.

- On the subject of non-standard usage of language, however, teachers are normally expected to use Standard English; so how can we explain the use of a singular standard against the linguistic reality outside the classroom?

- The classroom can be an ideal place to educate students about the linguistic diversity in the world and in doing so, help students to recognize the validity of all language varieties.

Do you know critical writing when you see it?

Have a look at the text below, based once again on the original paragraph presented in this section. You be the judge – do you think the writing below is evidence of being critical or not?

Teacher identity has been researched a great deal in the United States, especially in terms of language. Perhaps teachers do not wish to relinquish their home language when they teach their students. Are the expectations fair, however, for the teaching profession in terms of what is or is not 'appropriate' language? What makes a 'good' teacher? Is language an important part of this? Language use can also reflect one's racial identity.

Jot down your thoughts here:

....

....

....

....

....

A student told us

'You can't always know the author's intended meaning, but you can always show the reader your meaning.'

Are there different ways to understand interpretation?

10 second summary

The key to being critical – interpretation – is revealed on several different levels, all of which can be combined in your assessments to reveal criticality.

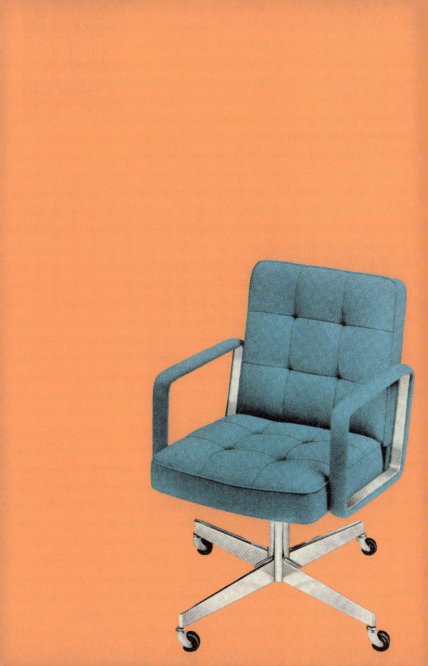

60 second summary

Interpretation is the name of the game when it comes to being critical

Again, interpretation of the source material is the key to demonstrating criticality so read critically (interpret the material), to then activate critical thinking which is then transferred to your assessment. However, 'interpretation' can itself be interpreted in different ways, and below are examples which demonstrate this. In each case, the same source text is used as the means to then display criticality. This shows how versatile a text can really be, in that not only can we all interpret it differently, but also, we can approach interpretation itself from the variety of ways shown below: agreement, disagreement, illustration, and explanation. They differ in terms of content, but are otherwise the same in terms of showing criticality – different approaches to interpretation of the same text.

Approaches to interpretation

Below is a short text, for which each of the four approaches to interpretation is revealed. Namely:

1   Agreement
2   Disagreement
3   Illustration
4   Explanation

Illustration A concrete example of what is otherwise a broad concept, theory or term. This is especially useful as a means to demonstrate that you truly understand the subject, provided your illustrations are yours of course, and not a cut and paste from lecture notes/class discussion.

Text (by 'John Doe', 2019)

Our natural, unmodified accent is arguably the most authentic indicator of linguistic identity, in that its unmodified nature suggests that we are simply 'being ourselves'. However, we need to consider the perceptions others have with regard to certain accents in the UK. If our accent is generally perceived negatively within society, it is conceivable that we might seek to modify it, more so when in social settings in which our natural accent would be especially prone to judgement; not wanting to be seen in a negative light can therefore contribute to shaping our linguistic identity.

1/ Agreement

Doe's (2019) comments about accent are indeed relevant. It is entirely conceivable that even in this day and age, certain regional accents are perceived negatively. As such, for those who speak with such accents in professional contexts such as teaching, for example, the price they might have to pay for being perceived as 'professional' may indeed involve toning down the more regional sounds in their accents.

My comments:

I think that some students believe that disagreeing with an author is somehow synonymous with being critical. The key to being critical is not whether you agree or disagree with what you read. Instead, it is about *how you explain* why you do or do not agree. Therefore, the above paragraph is displaying criticality precisely because it takes the time to explore the validity of Doe's statement and to do this, it stands to reason that the author who agrees with Doe must have taken some time to stop and think first.

> 'There are different ways to interpret what you read, so choose a few to suit you – variety is the spice of life, and assessments.'

2/ Disagreement

While Doe (2019) makes a valid point about the negative attitudes that still exist toward certain accents, there is ample evidence that accent diversity in Britain is alive and well and as such, we see more celebration of different accents than ever before. Given the regional variations heard on the BBC, for example, and celebrities who refuse to modify their accents, it is perhaps unsurprising that this linguistic defiance can be seen within everyday life.

My comments:

The disagreement shows critical thinking skills because, once again, the writer is taking the time to explain and explore the reasons why he/she does not (totally) agree with Doe's stance. Moreover, in doing so, the writer is also building his/her own argument, implied with the term *linguistic defiance*. This suggests that individuals are not afraid to use their otherwise unmodified accents, as opposed to letting the potential negative perceptions of others affect their use of language.

3/ Illustration

Doe makes the comment that certain British accents, no matter how proud the 'owner' might be, can nonetheless come up against negative perceptions by others within British society. For example, while Received Pronunciation was for a long time the 'standard' British accent and still enjoys a degree of respectability, it can also be the case that speakers of accents perceived as 'posh' might be regarded as aloof and arrogant. Equally at fault, however, are attitudes toward broad accents tied to the North, often perceived by some as 'common' and leading to snap judgements about the speaker's class- and education-level. It is these ideas in particular which might lead to the perception of some individuals not being a good 'fit' for certain professions such as banking and teaching, unfair though such a perception is.

My comments:

I mentioned the need to ensure that you take the time to illustrate broad words and statements. Otherwise, your writing will sound abstract and even hard to fathom. But the use of an illustration for such words can help to make your writing more concrete. In the example above, the writer takes the time to give an example which readers can probably relate to, if not on a personal level then certainly based on general knowledge. The illustration offered is quite specific, in terms of providing a social context in which people might wish to adjust their language use, and thus provides a specific illustration of Doe's reference to the otherwise broad term of 'social settings'.

4/ Explanation

Doe (2019) is taking the subject of accent and perhaps expanding it to go beyond merely pronunciation. Instead, he is discussing the *societal connotations* of accent, which can of course be positive or negative. It is suggested that the central issue here is not necessarily how individuals feel about their own accents – important though that is – but more about how other people feel about individuals' accents. The clear implication is that, given a desire perhaps to fit within societal settings, accent modification may be a reality. As much as individuals may like, even celebrate their accent, they may not wish to be perceived by others as any less than they are.

My comments:

What is happening in the example above is the writer is making the implications of Doe's work relevant to the reader. Therefore, the writer is stretching out Doe's original reference to societal attitudes and expanding on this. In doing so, the writer shows criticality because he/she has taken the original work and gone further with it, revealing his/her own insights in the process. As you can also see, there is no agreement or disagreement with Doe. In fact, what could follow this explanation is the writer making his/her feelings on the matter clear, in terms of agreeing, or disagreeing, with Doe. But for now, the writer has offered some clear interpretation of the original text, by means of explaining it as he/she sees fit.

Summary

As you can see, there are four examples of how to approach 'interpretation' and perhaps you can think of others, or even combine one or two of the approaches above. The key factor in all of these approaches, however, is that **they all add something new**. The writers use the original text as a launching pad from which to then bring in their own original ideas. Once again, having something new to say within your interpretation of the text is the crux to being critical and it all begins with the reading.

A student
told us

'Mix and match the various ways to show interpretation skills for a well-rounded approach to being critical.'

CHECK POINT Can you choose an approach to interpretation?

- Critically examine the short text below.

- Then, decide on one of the four critical approaches discussed in this section.

- Use your chosen approach to demonstrate your critical understanding of Einstein's quote.

Einstein said there are two ways to live your life. One is as though nothing is a miracle. The other is as though everything is a miracle.

Type of Interpretation:

....

Interpretation:

....

....

....

....

....

....

....

....

Congratulations

By now, you should understand the following:

- How to approach interpretation.

- Being critical is not always about disagreeing with authors.

- Doing nothing with the literature, and merely providing quotes for quotes' sake, is not critical enough; doing something with the quote/reference is!

What is critical language?

10 second
summary

Critical language reflects the fact you have considered your propositions, opinions and assertions; thus, you don't seek to make them sound too ambitious, but reflect a degree of doubt instead.

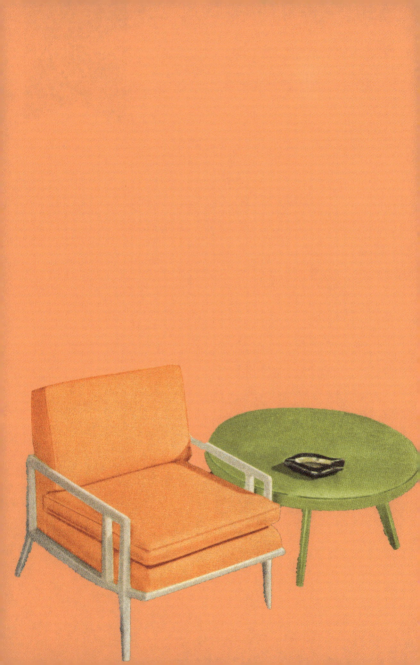

60 second summary

You might be certain of your points, but never let it show!

We've discussed critical writing (or speaking, for oral assessments) as the final destination for your analytical skills. This is where you demonstrate to lecturers your understanding of the subject matter, because they will never have a direct window into how you read or think. But indirectly they will, seen with how well you communicate your ideas as part of your assessments. To do so effectively, make sure you communicate your ideas in language that is cautious rather than bold. This is part of a practice called 'hedging', which is very important in academic circles, and especially within your assessments.

Hedging in different academic disciplines

To get started, first have a good look at the sentence below:

This proves that Freud's beliefs are valid.

Can you spot the one word which might raise a red flag? It is the word 'proves' of course, because it communicates a very powerful message: that something is a fact. First of all, consider the academic community for which you write. The Hard Sciences (Chemistry, Physics) are indeed focused on facts, which means that otherwise 'cautious' language is not generally required as much. The sciences communicate facts by use of the present tense, for example, so that *the sun rises in the East* is essentially saying, *it is a fact that the sun rises in the East*. Clearly, there is no need to hedge here: *Arguably, the sun rises in the East*.

> **Hedging** The practice of using cautious language in your academic assessments, in order to show reasoned conclusions and interpretations of the literature.

The Social Sciences, such as Linguistics and Psychology, are not tied to facts as such, given that their focus on people, cultures and communities is not perhaps as generalisable as natural phenomena that are often the focus of the Hard Sciences. Therefore, here is where we would start to expect more use of hedging, including words such as *might, perhaps, suggests* and so on.

The Humanities, such as Art and Literature, are the most interpretive of all academic communities. After all, people will interpret a book, painting or film in entirely different ways. In fact, given the inherently interpretive nature of this community, I would say that those who study here have a head start of sorts with critical thinking. When a Literature student, for example, who has been reading (and thus interpreting) poetry, plays and fiction since childhood arrives at university, he/she is already well prepared for the critical thinking that lies ahead within assessments.

But getting back to the example, do you think Freud's beliefs (whatever beliefs they might be), as part of the study of Psychology, have been proven? If so, how can we test that his beliefs are indeed facts? To be considered a fact, we would need to conduct perhaps a worldwide survey, for example. But this is not practical at all. Thus, rather than use the word 'prove', the word *suggests* fits much better. This word does not assert itself and in fact means that you, as the writer, could be wrong. But in showing a degree of doubt for your claims, opinions and interpretations, you will be taken more seriously as a writer.

Hedging practice

Now consider the sentence pairs below:

Doe's (2019) research proves that wind energy is the best way forward.

Doe's (2019) research suggests that wind energy might be the best way forward.

Based on the results of my study, it is clear that bilingual education is essential for all schools.

Based on the results of my study, it is clear that bilingual education is desirable for some schools in particular.

The research provides the most updated perspective on linguistic policy.

Arguably, the research provides the most updated perspective on linguistic policy.

Can you see, and appreciate, the difference a word (e.g. 'arguably') can make? It can be the difference between sounding like a novice and sounding like an academic. So, situate yourself with regard to the discipline in which you are studying, but remember that all academic disciplines, to a greater or lesser extent, rely on hedging.

'Showing doubt in your writing is a strength, and showing absolute certainty is a weakness.'

ACTIVITY What is appropriate academic language?

Read the statements below and decide if they are true or false:

Providing an opinion within my writing is one sign of
being confident.   True / False

Using cautious language means that I am
less confident.   True / False

Using cautious language could win me the respect of
the reader.   True / False

It's possible to be 100% certain about my views, but
still use cautious language.   True / False

Making over the top claims and assertions could
sound a bit immature.   True / False

CHECK POINT Hedge your bets

Consider the following text. Can you edit it in order to make it more academic, in terms of adding hedged language (and perhaps deleting overly assertive language too)?

Social media marketing is an absolutely integral element of 21st-century business. However, the literature on social media marketing is positively fragmented and is focused on isolated issues, such as tactics for effective communication. The current research applies a qualitative, theory-building approach to develop a strategic framework that articulates four generic dimensions of strategic social media marketing. Social media marketing scope represents a range from defenders to explorers, social media marketing culture includes the poles of conservatism and modernism, social media marketing structures fall between hierarchies and networks, and social media marketing governance ranges from autocracy to anarchy. By providing a comprehensive conceptualization and definition of strategic social media marketing, this research proves the merit of an integrative framework that expands beyond extant marketing theory. Furthermore, if managers apply the framework to position their organizations on these four dimensions in a manner consistent with their overall corporate mission and objectives, their businesses will undoubtedly succeed.

Source: Taken and adapted from Felix, Rauschnabel and Hinsch (2017: 118)

Write down your revisions here:

....

....

....

....

....

....

....

....

....

....

....

....

....

A student
told us

'No one is impressed with a bragger, so don't brag
in your writing.'

How do I know I'm ready for the next assignment?

10 second summary

Thinking is important, but so is trusting your instincts.

60 second summary

Being critical is certainly predictable

Though you have the knowledge you already need, it's not enough to simply store it away in your head. Instead, you need to test drive it. While there have been examples and exercises throughout this guide to improve your ability in being critical, this section is devoted to providing a run-through. It is separated into three parts: (critically) reading the assignment directive, gathering your (critical) thoughts on the matter and then presenting a (critical) write-up. While I provide some prompts, it is otherwise all down to you. You know how to approach the act of being critical, so here you have a chance to do so in a systematic way.

> 'There is no perfect time to
> write – just work with what you have
> and go back to it later.'

STEP ONE: INTERPRET THE QUESTION

Discuss the connection between the Me Too Movement and the current films of Hollywood.

You might think that there's no connection between films and a societal movement. If just reading the sentence, probably not. But after giving it some analysis, you might just re-think that. There is something to be found if you look closely.

Discuss – Consider, and write down, what this word means in the context of academic assessment, based on what was discussed previously.

The connection – Even an article (a, the) can make a difference in perception. What is the difference between 'a connection' and 'the connection'?

Me Too Movement – Consider the use of capital letters beyond merely acting as a means to designate this movement as 'official'. Might the use of capital letters have any other function?

Current films of Hollywood – Do you define 'current' as films made since the start of the Me Too Movement? This would make sense. You're free to choose your own specific time line as long as it includes films which, to your understanding (and subsequent analysis), demonstrate a link with a movement focused on female empowerment. Also, you would clearly need to reference a few films; and further, how many films are sufficient to represent 'Hollywood' in relation to the Me Too Movement – how many films represent 'a few' (this is partly based on the word count for the assignment)? Also, don't forget the focus is on

Hollywood. For this reason, even a great British movie which deals with the movement would not be relevant to your discussion, unless it is indeed a Hollywood-produced film (e.g. produced by Universal, Paramount, etc.) set in Britain. This is the kind of micro-level – call it picky if you like – analysis that is needed throughout.

Again, you might not think there is a connection, but that is precisely why critical thinking is needed. I recall seeing *Halloween* (2018), which was likened to female empowerment by some film critics, considering the female lead is fighting back against a masked killer forty years after she first encountered him. Yes, it's a horror film and fictitious and even if the creative team behind it were not thinking of any societal movement when they put it together, this doesn't stop you from finding a link to such. Also, considering films are so interpretive in nature to begin with, then it is entirely up to you how you see things. Interpretations of any kind of text are usually beyond our control anyway; we see what, and how, we see.

Additional (recent and/or up and coming) films to consider:

Wonder Woman 2

Bombshell

Working Woman

A personal thought ...

Of course, you could be really critical and choose current fims which, on the surface at least, do not appear to deal with the relevant aspects of the Me Too Movement. I remember watching *Titanic* and focusing in on the class issues – which might be fairly obvious. But taking the class issues within the film and applying a Marxist perspective to my analysis of *Titanic* might, at first glance, seem less obvious. Perhaps. But such a reading would be justifiable.

STEP TWO: DO SOME CRITICAL THINKING

This step involves pondering the question and its various parts, mulling it all over and arriving at an understanding. From here, you then provide evidence of critical writing. Use my brief prompts above regarding the key words of the assignment brief – you can then expand on these if you haven't done so already. Jot down some notes of your own and even better, come up with your own ideas and prompts.

Critical writing The act of putting evidence of your critical thinking down on paper, as part of an exam or essay assignment.

STEP THREE: CRITICAL WRITING

Try now to put together a rough draft. This doesn't mean a full essay, complete with literature. Rather, a single paragraph will suffice. It could be an introduction paragraph or a paragraph that is intended to come later on in the essay. Enough to show evidence of having interpreted a film of your choice perhaps, in line with the movement, or perhaps a paragraph which unpacks the movement as background information, to help set the scene. There is more than one approach. The key, as always, is to bring your personal understanding to the table.

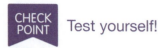
By now, you should be able to approach the three-part process of criti-cality: critical reading – critical thinking – critical writing.

For this exercise, select a sentence, or indeed a small paragraph of text, which you have taken from any source (online news report, magazine, etc.). Write the text below:

....

....

....

....

....

You know what to do next – read it critically:

• Circle the words which you believe are key.

• Interpret these – what do they mean to you?

Now prepare a short response to the original text consisting of your interpretation – agreement, disagreement, illustration, explanation, or all of the above – regarding the original text.

....

....

....

....

....

OK. Time to take a break! Close the book and come back to it at least half an hour later.

Had a break? Good. Look over your work one more time. Are you satisfied with it? If not, consider any ways that you can improve it and make the changes below:

....

....

....

....

....

A student told us

'Before submitting your assessment, revise, revise, revise'

Where do I go from here?

10 second summary

You know where to go – back to the beginning with each and every future assignment: critically read the question and critically read the relevant literature; then, gather your thoughts.

60 second
summary

A final reminder ...

For each and every assessment, the approach is the same to criticality, no matter the type of assessment. Remember the golden rules when it comes to demonstrating criticality in your assessments. Interpret the data – whatever form that takes – and make sure that your interpretation is, as far as you can tell, yours and yours alone. This doesn't mean that you have to stress yourself, worrying about whether or not your interpretation is the only one of its kind. Instead, just make sure that you know it's not a copy of what you've been told in class or given on a handout; instead, let your interpretations derive from such. The more you do this, the more your reader will see that you are taking charge of your assessments and above all your knowledge, and this is what gets you the higher scores.

Good luck!

ACTIVITY Some final exercises

Below is a collection of exercises which you can use to address the various components of criticality that have been discussed:

Exercise One: Can you spot the **broad word** in the sentence below and write it down? Don't forget – such words within your own writing need to be illustrated. Your teacher will not know what you mean unless you make it clear.

It is common for infants' language to display errors when acquiring their first language.

....

....

....

Exercise Two: Having identified the broad word in the sentence above, can you give an illustration – an example to help the reader understand a broad word in concrete terms?

....

....

....

Exercise Three: Do you think the second sentence below provides **an adequate illustration** of the first sentence? Explain.

There are many ways to achieve success in business. One such way is to first find a gap within the field you wish to succeed in.

....

....

....

Exercise Four: Can you provide **an interpretation** (of any kind) of the sentence below?

Smith (2000) argues that for globalization to truly work, its benefits must reach the smallest village.

....

....

....

Exercise Five: Can you identify **the key words** in the assignment brief below?

Discuss the ways in which climate change is possibly affecting tourism.

....

....

....

Exercise Six: Now, can you provide a short summary of the meaning/ implications/connotations of these key words in relation to the overall purpose of the assignment?

....

....

....

Exercise Seven: Can you identify which of the following three sentences is **most trustworthy in tone**?

1   The research proves that immediate solutions are needed to address current water scarcity in megacities.

2   The research strongly suggests that solutions are needed soon to address current water scarcity in megacities.

3   The research implies that at some point, we will need to find solutions to address current water scarcity in megacities.

Write number here: _____

Exercise Eight: Critically read the writing sample below and adjust the language to make it sound **more cautious** – and thus, more critical in its tone:

Everyone agrees that equality in society is important. Therefore, it is important that we consider equality on all levels for all people. This can be seen not only in the workplace, for example, but also by how we treat people throughout our day, from strangers waiting for the bus, to people who give us directions. It is vital that we do not lose sight of the need to treat everyone as an equal, regardless of race, ethnicity or religion, or anything else. This is a fact.

....

....

....

Exercise Nine: Read the sentence below and explain why or why not it could be seen as both convincing *and* unconvincing:

Children of the British Royal Family would never be given non-traditional names such as Steve and Debbie.

....

....

....

Exercise Ten: Read the sentence below and explain the effect of the quote marks around the expression. How do these marks affect your perception of the expression?

Each of us has his or her unique 'linguistic fingerprints'.

....

....

....

'For each and every assessment, the approach is the same to criticality, no matter the type of assessment.'

Final checklist: How to know you are done

Do you understand the difference between merely reading a text and *critically* reading it?... Yes / No

Do you understand how to actually *do* critical reading?.............. Yes / No

Do you feel more knowledgeable now with regard to how to approach an assignment question? .... Yes / No

Do you know how to approach the act of critical thinking once you have critically read a text – can you gather your thoughts? .... Yes / No

Crucially, do you know how to put your thoughts down on paper for your assignment – can you communicate your critical thinking effectively?.. Yes / No

Do you feel confident in your ability to mix and match the various strategies for interpreting the source text?..................... Yes / No

Do you know how to avoid assertive statements and replace them with more appropriate, hedged language? .... Yes / No

A student told us

'Get in the habit of ticking boxes, as this will inform much of your approach to quality writing for your assessments.'

Glossary

Analysis   The act of investigating key words (for texts) and the overall meaning derived, in order to find a deeper meaning and/or the implications of the text.

Assessment   The means by which your knowledge of a subject is tested at university, including essays, exams and oral presentations, for example.

Criticality   This is largely the same as analysis above, involving the need for close reading, probing for meaning and leading to the presentation of your own insights and interpretation.

Critical reading   The act of not just reading a text, but asking questions about it – the implications for the claims it makes, considering examples of such claims and overall, trying to come to a central point – an interpretation – of the content.

Critical speaking   Communicating in speech (e.g. for an oral assessment) the evidence of your critical thinking (see below).

Critical thinking   The act of pondering over the text as you read, or after reading, in order to reach an overall interpretation.

Critical writing   The act of putting evidence of your critical thinking down on paper, as part of an exam or essay assignment.

Evaluation   The act of interpreting a source text in terms of what it's implying, not what it's necessarily saying directly; this involves reading between the lines which, of course, ties in with critical reading.

Hedging   The practice of using cautious language in your academic assessments, in order to show reasoned conclusions and interpretations of the literature.

Illustration   A concrete example of what is otherwise a broad concept, theory or term. This is especially useful as a means to demonstrate that you truly understand the subject, provided your illustrations are yours of course, and not a cut and paste from lecture notes/class discussion.

Interpretation   Coming up with your own opinions based on the content of the text you've read.

Reading   The act of simply reading a text in front of you and nothing more.

Text   The source material from which a critical reading – and understanding – derives, such as a book, journal article, painting, film, picture and so on.

Further reading and resources

Baratta, A. (2019). Academic writing goes to the movies. Getting critical in your essays. Amazon Kindle.

Critical thinking and reflection – Learn Higher. www.learnhigher.ac.uk/learning-at-university/critical-thinking-and-reflection/

The Open University critical thinking guide. www.openuniversity.edu/sites/www.openuniversity.edu/files/brochures/Critical-thinking-Open-University.pdf

UCAS Study skills guides. www.ucas.com/undergraduate/student-life/study-skills-guides